Copyright © 2016

J. C. Bellerive

This book and its contents are protected under copyright laws of the United States and other countries. The characters and story conception of this book in partial or in whole are copyright. All rights reserved.

ISBN-10: 1530397685
ISBN-13: 978-1530397686

The Adventures of

Ajax and Alexander

Previously…

Sighing quietly, Ajax sat back slowly against the side of her bed. She breathed in a deep breath. Looking down at Alexander she smiled and then asked him, "Okay Alexander, where to next?"

The morning was still very young following Ajax and Alexander's earlier adventure together to ancient Australia. It was an adventure that Ajax will never forget.

During that first journey, Ajax had learned some of the history of the Aborigines of Australia. She learned about how they lived forty-thousand years ago and about their culture from the past. She ate some of the foods they hunted and gathered from that time as well as witnessed a communal gathering with songs, music, and discussions. She even picked up a few words of their spoken language.

Today, the bright patches of sunlight meandered across her bedroom carpet. The sunlight now shone through Ajax's open bedroom curtain painting golden yellow bars on her bedroom floor.

She looked at her clock again. On their last adventure and the first one together, she realized that it had only taken one minute of real time. This amazed Ajax and left her with many questions about time travel.

At this moment however, neither of them had made a decision on where to go next when suddenly there was a surprising knock on Ajax's bedroom door.

Ajax answered as she quickly stowed Alexander under the bed.

"Yes?" She questioned.

It was her brother, Austin.
He opened the door slightly and said, "Mom and Dad want us all to have lunch at Willie's Diner today. So if you go out, be back by noon."

"Sounds good," Ajax replied.

Willie's Diner was the place to be on a Saturday morning. A lot of the town's folks would be there talking about the events from their past week. It was a central meeting place for most of the people around the town. There would be news, gossip, but most of all, lots of good food. It was a great gathering place for families and friends to just hang out before beginning their day.

Ajax especially enjoyed the breakfasts there. The flap jacks with fresh butter and maple syrup melted in your mouth. And with some hash browns, eggs, and bacon or sausage on the side, well this just started off your day wonderfully.

But, she'd settle for a nice Willie's double cheese burger anytime. "Um, yummy," she thought. And don't forget a side of slaw and some fries smothered with catsup and a large chocolate shake to wash it all down.

Ajax realized that she was getting hungry already. Even though she had breakfast a couple of hours ago, the thought of Willie's food made her crave more.

Austin replied, "Okay," as he closed her bedroom door and headed up the hall to his room. He was unaware that Morpheus the cat had quickly scurried through the slightly opened door before it shut closed.

Morpheus is the family pet. Actually, one of several pets living with Ajax and her family. He is a very large cat with short calico colored fur and he thinks he is running the entire family. He is named after the Greek god of dreams that mimics humans and other creatures.

In fact, about a year ago, Morpheus showed up at their back door without a name tag or collar. They put out flyers and even a note in the paper about his whereabouts, but no one had responded. So they decided to keep him.

He quickly scurried underneath Ajax's bed. Ajax was still sitting on the floor as she turned and reached under her bed for Alexander, just missing Morpheus' nose. She had not noticed Morpheus enter her room when she responded to Austin earlier.

She began to wonder now if someone would have entered her room while she and Alexander were away on an adventure would they not be able to see them. Or, would they be like statues, physically there, but not moving?

As Ajax pulled Alexander onto her lap Alexander immediately retorted, "There is no need to put me under your bed, in the dark you know."

"I know, Alexander, sorry about that. It was like, just a reaction. I'm not ready for anyone to see you, let alone share you with anyone." She replied apologetically.

He responded, "You need to understand that to everyone else I just look like some old broken, dirty, and nonfunctioning laptop."

"In fact Ajax, you should keep me out so that everyone around you becomes accustom to seeing you and me together. I look this way on purpose and for a reason. It is important that I do not fall into the wrong person's hands. My rubbished appearance is deliberate and causes many observers to lose interest as soon as they see my ugly appearance."

Ajax replied, "Okay. I'll remember that."

"So Alexander, do you have any ideas on where we should go to next?" Ajax questioned.

He remained quiet to allow Ajax some time on her own, to come up with a decision on where they should travel next.

"Hum," She thought for a minute and then asked him, "What do you think about Stonehenge and the ancient Druids of England? I have always been amazed at that place and have never been there. And the Druids, they are so mystical and full of knowledge."

Alexander replied, "Ah yes, Stonehenge. It is located in Wiltshire on Salisbury Plain, England, just west of Amesbury."

Ajax replied, "Um, I believe that's where it is."

All she could recall was that Salisbury Plain sounded familiar to what she had read and understood about Stonehenge's location.

Then Ajax questioned him off-the-cuff. She asked, "Hey Alexander, why the silence earlier?"

Alexander replied, "Oftentimes I am updating my knowledge data banks with newly acquired information. This is a continual event. I do my best to perform any maintenance or updates when I am not in use. However, there is so much information in the universe that is continually changing that it is difficult to keep up to date.

In this particular case I was allowing you time and the opportunity to explore your thoughts, your knowledge, and interests to come up with our next adventure on your own. This will be our common practice."

"Oh," Ajax replied adding, "Okay then. Continuing with my earlier question, how about Stonehenge? That is one place that has always interested me. It was built without modern machinery or tools and the rocks are huge!"

Ajax confidently continued lecturing, "It was built between four to five thousand years ago and construction began by nomadic gatherers around 2400 B.C. It is believed that it took over one thousand years to complete. There were many stages through its completion."

"After final construction the Druids of Britain were the last to occupy Stonehenge, but only for short time, because the Romans conquered the Druids during the expansion of the Roman Empire. The Romans are blamed for much of the destruction to this wonderful site as we see what is left standing today."

"It did take the Romans some time to conquer the Druids because of what they saw and heard of the Druids around the area."

"It is believed and known that the Druids performed sacrifices, rituals, and were educated. At the time they realized the Romans were on their way, the Druids would have placed scarecrows of the dead tied tightly to supports. Some of these were beheaded while other victims were deliberately left suspended upside down."

"There were other scary things set out for Roman soldiers to see and fear."

"The Druids continued to try everything they knew to try to please the gods to avoid capture, even sacrificing their very own. But this too eventually failed and the Romans captured and killed most if not all of the Druids they got their hands on."

Alexander jumped in adding, "There remain only seventeen Sarsen stones. These are the really big ones that make up the giant trilithons we see today. Originally, there were thirty of these massive stones. They are the tall upside down u-shaped giant stones. Some of these massive stones weigh up to forty tons each. This is as much weight as a fully loaded semi truck."

"It is believed that the ancients built many of these rock-related sites all around England and Europe from massive stones deliberately. It was because to them anything large represented that there is something bigger out there, something bigger than mankind."

Ajax then added, "It is amazing at how such primitive cultures could perform these great feats without the use of modern tools and by using only rolling sleds, antlers and rock tools in the beginning of Stonehenge."

"But to be honest with you, I believe that we don't give our ancient ancestors credit for the abilities they had, especially with large numbers of people." She concluded.

Alexander was surprised at how smart Ajax was in regards to Stonehenge.

He responded, "Very nice. When you are ready we will depart. I think that I will surprise you on the time period that we shall visit this marvel of prehistoric engineering."

Ajax thought for a little while longer and then answered him, "How about we visit there at the end of the completed version, when Stonehenge was in its magnificence and complete?"

"Oh, hold on," Ajax shouted!

She quickly placed Alexander on the floor off to her side, got up and quickly gathered up her socks and shoes that she had haphazardly scattered around her room when she first sat down this morning the previous time.

She quickly fumbled her socks back on; having to twist both heals around on each foot in order for them to fit and feel right. She then put her shoes over them and on the correct feet!

She reached for Alexander and looking at her clock so she could make a mental note of the time, she said, "Ok Alexander, I am ready."

She was also surprised from their first adventure that the hands on the clock did not move backwards as she had seen in movies. This was probably for the visual affect for them to be moving backwards. For her however, as soon as the adventure started everything faded away.

She could not believe that only a minute of real time had passed during their previous overnight excursion to prehistoric Australia. She and Alexander had spent a day and a night back in time in Australia, yet only a minute of 'her' time had passed.

Nothing happened immediately.

Silence filled the room. Nothing was going on. There was no blur of things around the room, no sparkles of light and color.

"So, why aren't we moving, Alexander?" She questioned with some concern in her voice.

Alexander said to her, "On our first adventure we were involved in, I decided to perform a demonstration of what I can do going only by the information I had gathered by scanning around your room. From now on however, we will make our decisions based on the choices we make together."

"Gotcha," she replied.

Ajax then asked, "So, how does this work? Do I have to push a button or type in a specific word or phrase that starts the process?" She looked frantically around Alexander's keyboard. Then, she looked underneath and all around him, picking him up and turning him over.

"Ajax, stop, stop, you are making me dizzy."

He continued, "As we become more familiar with one another, I should be able to pick up on which time you want us to travel to. Also, as we become more in tuned with one another, I will actually react to your thoughts and touch without you even saying a word. It is really quite amazing how this all works. It will all come in time."

"Time… he, he," Alexander chuckled electronically.

Ajax smiled back and replied, "Okay, I'm ready. Let's do this."

"Yes, my Lady. Four thousand two hundred years ago it is. Now just close my top and hold on."

Ajax followed his directions.

There was an immediate brilliance. Things around Ajax's room began to sparkle and light up in many colored hues of glowing light. Her eyes quickly lost focus of her surroundings; however, she did manage to take one last peek at her bedroom clock before it twinkled out of sight.

Only fifteen minutes had passed since their last return as they had sat and talked in her room.

And with that, everything blurred.

Under the bed,  Morpheus had observed everything.

Ajax closed her eyes quickly.

In an instant she felt like her back was still leaning against her bed, or so she thought.

She blinked her eyes a few times as they adjusted and then glanced to her left and then to her right. But to her surprise she was no longer leaning against her bed or in her room, but she was now leaning back against a cold giant stone!

She shot up from the hard grassy ground and shot up quickly with Alexander in her hands.

Stepping back further she looked around excitedly at the amazing sight that towered before her.

She was now standing on the outside of Stonehenge, out past the outer ring of trilithons that encircled the site.

Ajax slowly turned herself around to take a look at the surroundings and then returned her stare at the stone that she was leaning against previously.

The stones were gigantic and as tall as a house.

They towered above her with the monolithic sarsen trilithons poking even higher above the outer stones.

Ajax stumbled back a few more steps backwards to get a better look in an attempt to see the whole thing.

"Oh my," she wondered aloud, looking right and left.

She was speechless but finally said to Alexander in excitement, "We are actually here. We are really at Stonehenge!" A great smile of joy stretched across her face.

Alexander replied softly, "Yes."

Ajax looked around in awe of everything she was seeing.

There were groups of people all around them. Some were busy setting up structures and setting camp fires while others were dressed in what reminded Ajax of the dully-colored, multi-layered renaissance period attire that she would see people wearing while visiting the county Renaissance Fair that was held every year in her county.

There were many people rushing around the monument itself. Some of these people consisted of families with children and each had small fires lit as if marking their personal spot. There were things cooking on these fires, fish and fowl, meats of all kinds and many with suspended cauldrons hanging from crisscrossed posts with steam rising from their open tops. Some of these groupings had tents while others had more extravagant temporary structures build further back from the site.

Ajax moved forward and attempted to peer into inside of Stonehenge. With much difficulty, she soon realized that the current arrangement of stones in Stonehenge had purposely been designed to prevent someone from seeing all the way in as well as from seeing directly out. This is with exception to the view of the Heel Stone.

As she peered inside she realized that the trilithons and the shorter blue stones prevented her eyes from seeing directly into the center. There were sixty of these originally and those standing were blocking her view. These blue stones we quarried from the Preseli Mountains, about twenty miles away.

At that time, she then recalled from her readings that Stonehenge seemed to be deliberately designed so that any person on the outside trying to look in could not easily see to the center. Just as well as when a person was on the inside they could not see out very easily to the outside of the monument. This must be for a reason, but she did not understand why at this moment.

Ajax also recalled that sound was an important feature to this shrine.

She recalled that there were experiments conducted using sound waves and how some pitches were magnified while others were stifled and barely audible or heard.

Stonehenge could be used as a musical auditorium, or be as silent as a subterranean cave.

A large crowd started milling all around the outside of the site. There were men, women, and a few children. The children seemed to pay little attention to whatever was going to happen. They spent most of their time just running around and pretty much annoying their elders.

Ajax could see a couple of men moving about inside of the shrine. It seemed to her that all of them were busy undergoing some kind of preparation for something to occur later in the day. All of these men were wearing long white robes. One of them seemed to be the one in charge because he was giving directions to the others. Also, his robe was highly decorated with flashy ornaments that reflected the sunlight that shown down from above.

Ajax conducted an experiment of her own. She wanted to test a theory that she had just thought of.

She recalled from her first adventure with Alexander in ancient Australia, that even though she was bare foot, she could walk over the hard crunchy ground without feeling a thing. Alexander explained this to her as since they were from a different time and not of the time period they were visiting, their presence was and at the same moment, was not. This is still very confusing to her.

He had also mentioned that she unknowingly was controlling her senses.

She did not quite understand why people could see them and interact with them, but yet they were from different times.

In any case, she wondered what if she thought about the temperature, the texture, and what surrounded her, could she then feel as well. Would the air around her be cold, as it appeared to be by seeing all the clothing that the people were wearing? If she were to touch one of the stones, would it be cool or cold to the touch?

She thought to herself that maybe if she thought about cold or hot, or soft or hard, would her senses become active and would she be able to feel?

Ajax also recalled that while in the outback of Australia, she could hear animal sounds and smell the aromas of things cooking on a fire. Was this because she thought of these things? Is it that only when she thinks of being seen, they are seen?

She then paused for a second and breathed in a long slow breath. She wanted to see if she could smell anything immediately. And then, if she thought hard enough could she make herself not smell anything? Could she control her senses in time travel?

Immediately, she could smell the smoke from the fires. She could feel the cold air rush through her nose. There was an earthy scent mixed with a smell of oil, possibly from torches being lit as a tiny sun was setting lower in the west horizon.

She felt a chill suddenly. Then she got even colder. She looked at her arms and noticed what she was wearing. She was not dressed for this type of weather she was now a part of.

Quickly she realized that she needed to control this or she would soon freeze.

With all of her concentration she closed her eyes and cleared her thoughts of the cold.

Immediately, her body slowly warmed. Even the cold and the smells in the air began to lessen.

Finally, she felt comfortable again and realized that she will need to work on this and learn how and when to control all or some of her senses while on different adventures with Alexander.

As more crowd gathered, Ajax held Alexander tightly behind her arms.

The two of them moved slowly with the crowd around Stonehenge and stopped at a flat portion of the area.

The people all knew that Ajax was there, but none of them seemed to care. They all had something more important going on at the time.

Close by, Ajax watched as more torches became alight.

Ajax could also see more torch lights off in the distance all around the site.

She could hear the slow beating of animal skin drums, but she could not tell if the source for the sounds was coming from outside or from within Stonehenge itself.

A large crowd began to move slowly around the site to the rhythm of the drums. Ajax found herself and Alexander caught in this collection as they too moved clockwise around the monument.

A multitude of different aromas and scents were filling the air.

The low sounds from the drums continued.

Eventually, the two of them had walked around the perimeter of this amazing monument with the crowd. Then Alexander began to lecture to Ajax.

"Through archeological evidence; bones, tools, and other artifacts, it is believed that three different tribes or clans of people contributed to Stonehenge during its many centuries of changes and construction."

"The first to inhabit the area of the Salisbury Plain were the Neolithic people. They built circular hill top enclosures, including long barrows. These may have had woven cloth roofs or grass and moss covered roofs. Many of these are still seen today in the area all around us."

"These people used antler bones, axes and arrowheads made from stone and flint for their tools and equipment."

"They are responsible for the initial stages, the henge and ditch part to Stonehenge."

"This was a time of early agriculture, when organized and planned planting and harvesting became important. Seasonal timing was of the utmost importance to them."

"These Neolithic people raised domesticated animals like pigs and cattle also. It is believed that deliberate enclosures were used to maintain the larger herds of animals during this period."

"There has been no archeological evidence of this occurring before this time."

Ajax listened attentively as Alexander instructed.

She observed the crowd as it continued to move them along a second time.

She studied the crowd's movements, the way they carried themselves, and their facial expressions. Some danced and spun around while others just walked along.

The drums continued playing in rhythmic sounds.

Ajax's mind was like a sponge soaking up all this new knowledge that Alexander was presenting to her and of the things she was witnessing all around her.

Alexander continued talking as they walked and no one around them seemed to care or notice Alexander's voice when he spoke to Ajax.

This is because Alexander controlled everything and anything that had to do with him or Ajax being there.

Ajax did not know this at the time. Eventually this would all be shared with her.

They soon found themselves stopping with the crowd suddenly. Ajax bumped into the person on her left from the sudden stop.

"Sorry," she said softly, looking up at the guy she had bumped into. He just looked down at her, really not paying much attention to her.   It was as if his mind was on something else.

Alexander paused in his lecture to Ajax.

Before them stood two very long lines of people standing facing each other with a wide gap of grass between both line formations. Most of the people were standing and some of them were sitting.

Ajax pushed herself through the nearest thick line of people to see what was on the inside.

With some struggle, she made it through and saw a causeway, a road of land that stretched for quite some distance; past the village and across a vast field, down and then over to a river. It is often referred to as, The Avenue.

A light but steady chilling breeze blew up and across the avenue to where she stood; Ajax could feel its chill. Immediately, she put the cold breeze thought behind her in her mind. It worked.

Ajax could feel a coolness all around her now, but nothing that actually chilled her to where she felt cold. She could see the breath misting from some of the people as they exhaled. This told her that it must be a very cold time of year at this location.

She was learning very quickly on how to control her senses. She could empower or activate one or many of her senses at one time as she thought about them.

Time travel was amazing!

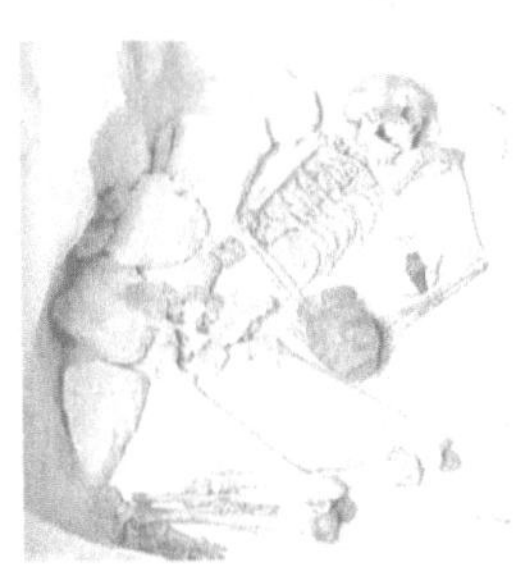

Alexander then started speaking to Ajax again.

"At the end of the Neolithic period, the Beaker people arrived. They are referred to Beaker people, because evidence of pottery beakers and cups has been discovered in the area and in some of their graves as well.”

“The Beakers exhibited a great reverence for their dead. They buried their dead using smaller graves consisting of only one or two family members buried alongside.”

“These were people that are thought to have worshipped the sun.”

“Because of this, it is believed that they rearranged the stones to align them in a more accurate manner to the summer and winter solstices.”

“This was also a time when the double circled blue stones were introduced to Stonehenge. They were also expert boatmen and this explains why and how the blue stones that were quarried and moved from hundreds of miles away.”

“They used mathematics as well as introducing additional metals which they used.”

“The Beakers introduced organized and community ways of living and also had chieftains that ruled over them.”

“Finally the Wessex people arrived. They were the third civilization to take part in the building of Stonehenge.”

"Evidence of bones and jewelry have been discovered in graves in the Stonehenge vicinity. The Wessex people were the most advanced of the three societies. To which we see before us today."

Alexander paused to allow Ajax time to absorb this new data and for her to comprehend it, not just hear it.

Ajax remained silent in thought. They had traveled back in time to around 2400 B.C. At a time when Stonehenge was bright and not discolored as it is today…and it looked amazing! The perimeter lintels were smooth and chiseled. Their color was bright and not dull.

Alexander added, "We are at a time when I thought you would get the most knowledge and experience as you had asked."

Ajax responded quickly looking down at Alexander, "Hey, how did you know what I was thinking?"

He added, "Let me remind you that we are becoming in-tune with one another. In a short amount of time I will be able to read most of your thoughts, but not all of them. Unfortunately, you will not be able to read my thoughts since they are not chemical-electrical as yours are. However, the foundational aspects to my processing are in electromagnetism. And as you get to know me and become more familiar with how I work, you will be able to anticipate some of my thoughts and actions before I think or perform them. But that will come in time."

"Let's head back to the monument. I want to examine it further if I can with all of these people here." Ajax suggested.

As they pushed their way through the ever growing crowd, Ajax began thinking out loud.

"There are one hundred and seventy-nine stones altogether. At least for now this is how many that have been discovered or unearthed. There are the sarsen stones and sixty of the Perseli blue stones from the Perseli Mountains about two hundred kilometers away. One of the blue stones is shorter than all the others and it is not understood exactly why, but it appears deliberately short for some reason."

She stopped. Then a great big smile stretched across Alex's face as she marveled at the magnificent sight standing before her. She shuttered inside a little bit.

She knew so much about this subject, and then she wondered if she should share any new knowledge she may see or learn, or should she keep these things to herself.

Maybe what she sees and learns is supposed to be discovered in its own time. This will be a conundrum that will haunt her from this moment on. That is, when or if

she should ever share any new unknown and
undiscovered evidence during any of her adventures.

Standing completely still, Ajax stared in awe at the
monolithic structure standing before her.
She was now directly in front of one of the massive
cold stones as she cautiously reached to touch it. Her
hand was trembling in anticipation to what she may or
may not feel.
At first her fingers slid along the smooth surface
very gently.
Pressing her hand a bit more firmly against the
stone, she began to feel its coldness.
A quick unexpected shiver quivered up from her
hand and through her arm. However, she did not move
and was not frightened. She quickly gave some thought
about this and the coolness dissipated.
She continued with her examination as Alexander
lay safely leaning against the bottom of the tremendous
stone in the grass and guarded by Ajax's feet.
He was almost completely hidden from the others.

The stone was chiseled, but pretty smooth for that
time period. The corner edges were delicately refined to
almost perfect ninety-degree angles. The lintel at the top
lay tightly upon the tips of the two large stones.
Together, the three stones made up one outer trilithon.

Between each and inside of the outer trilithons men stood holding torches. Some of the torches were already lit while others were not.

These giant men stood like enormous statues as if guarding something secret inside and that no one was allowed to see let alone enter. Unfortunately, this made it difficult for Ajax to get a good view of what was happening on the inside.

She looked around slowly at the people around her. Most of them had begun to settle down around the monument. More and more small fires began to pop up. A lot of the children were acting as normal kids do by running around making the best of what ever this event was for.

Ajax still did not know what was happening.

The evening was closing in.

Soon, the drumming echoed louder and the rhythm of the drumming increased.

Torchlight now became the greater source of light as the last of daylight had succumbed to the night.

A round silvery full moon slowly rose on the eastern horizon. Thousands of sparkling pin holes of starlight glistened from above. A brilliant Milky Way glowed as it snaked across the middle of the sky, showing its many different colors of white, black, orange and blue.

Suddenly, there was loud commotion coming from the avenue.

This alerted Ajax as she quickly reached down and grabbed Alexander from the ground. She grabbed him in such a hurry that several blades of grass ripped up from the earth within her hands as she pulled Alexander up quickly. Some of the blades of grass fell and clung onto her.

"When we are done here I really need to make something to hold you that will allow my hands to be free." She whispered loudly to him as they walked hastily towards the avenue again.

The large gathering also began moving towards the avenue also, making it difficult for Ajax to go in any other direction but forward.

She thought that this was okay though since they too wanted to go in that same direction anyway.

So like pebbles flowing down a moving mud slide, she and Alexander moved gracefully along with the crowd towards the avenue. They had no choice.

Soon, Ajax and Alexander were part of the mass of bodies that attacked at the near end of the avenue closest to Stonehenge. They were surrounded by even more people; all of them were taller than Ajax, so she could only see coat sleeves and shoulders that did not allow her any views what so ever.

Ajax quietly spoke to Alexander, "I'm going to try to work my way to the front of this thick line of people."

Alexander responded in a low pitched, beeping sound.

Twisting sideways, Ajax used her small size, elbow and shoulder to wedge herself through the living wall.

Within a minute, Ajax had managed to press herself forward enough to get to the front of the crowd. She stood sideways, but slowly and forcefully turned herself perpendicular to the exposed avenue.

As her eyes focused through the darkness she eventually spotted tiny light sources down the avenue and off into the distance. They were coming up from the river and slowly advancing towards where she stood.

The crowd roared loudly as more and more people noticed the procession entering the shore of the river's end of the avenue.

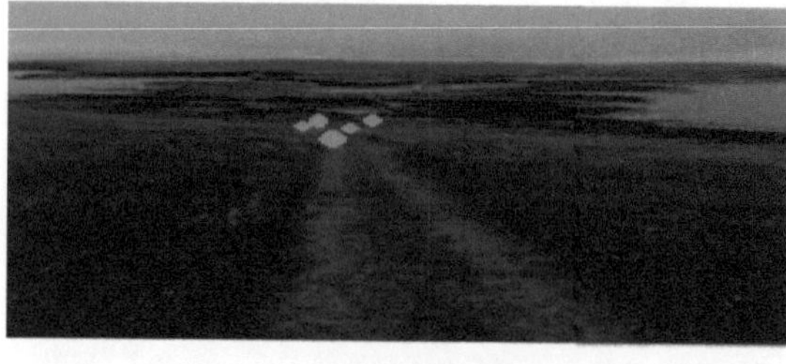

The scene was very eerie and dark and not a comfortable scene for Ajax. She was so glad she had Alexander with her and that he could probably easily get them out of a tight situation if necessary.

She was also concerned that because of the darkness of the night all was very dark. It did not help that the people had snuffed out all of their torches and fires for the time being.

She was thankful for the moonlight. It was now shining down on them.

Ajax thought, the snuffing of all light must have been done in order for everyone to observe the pageant that was slowly walking up towards Stonehenge.

Ajax concentrated now on both her smelling and hearing senses in order to get a good feel to this growing event. She was able to control how she felt the temperature of the air around her.

She really was getting quite good at this.

She watched in awe as the parade slowly drew closer and closer to where she stood. The lights from the advancing torches grew larger and brighter.

Now she could hear the pounding of drums beating slowly and loudly within the parade. Their rhythms shook and bounced off of the people lining the avenue as well as vibrating off of the ground.

Ajax's heart pounded hard inside her chest, almost in rhythm with the drums themselves. She felt herself becoming a part of this occasion as she heard the sounds, felt the people bumping against her, and by watching everything as it happened all around her.

She shook with excitement and thought, "What a marvelous thing happening right before my eyes. This is something that no one today could ever witness."

Alexander produced another "beep" sound, as if to acknowledge in agreement with what she was thinking and feeling.

She paused in her thoughts as she looked down at her hands that were holding him tightly. She wrinkled her forehead which was then followed with a smirk and a grin.

The drums pounded louder.

The advancing torches now lit up the area around her.

She could see excitement on many of the people's faces lit by the torch light. Many of them had their eyes wide open while others were sobbing, maybe in sadness or joy.

The people grew quiet now as the procession was slowly passed by Ajax as it crossed the henge and ditch, making its way towards Stonehenge.

Her eyes noticed darkly clothed and hooded men in the parade that were carrying something horizontally.

As they passed by her she saw what looked like a body wrapped tightly in cloth, and it was lying across wooden beams that the men were carrying at shoulder height. She thought of it like the pictures she had seen of medical stretchers used during war times.

Ajax then began to put together some of the pieces to this event.

She remembered reading about one theory that Stonehenge was a sacred sanctuary to the Druids and their people; it may have been used to honor the dead.

It represented the end. The end of life, but also the end of the winter and after the winter solstice the days would then become longer. This meant that the farmers could begin to prepare for planting season for the next year's crops.

Ajax gave more thought to all of the things going on tonight and she realized that maybe tonight was the twenty-first of December, the shortest day of the year, the winter solstice.

She whispered to herself, "The procession of the dead, the mysterious things happening inside of Stonehenge that no one was allowed to see at the moment, all of this had to do with tonight."

As the parade moved past Ajax the crowd re-lit all of the torches, candles, and campfires that were previously lit after the procession pasted by them.

The crowded line of people began shifting again as it followed the parade. This forced Ajax to have to move with it. She really did not have any choice but to follow along.

The collection of people of different shapes and sizes ambled their way closer to the monument.

She could now hear the drumming from within Stonehenge start up again as well as the drumming from the parade. The drums were in sequence with one another.

The sounds remained deep and earthy.

Ajax caught herself as they entered the outer edge of the henge, the ditch part of Stonehenge, just before she would have tripped and fallen in the ditch. If she had a torch in her hand she may have avoided it altogether. But she did not have a torch for lighting her way and she had to hold Alexander safely.

This got Ajax thinking again that maybe she could create a carrying bag that would hold Alexander, leaving her hands free. She'd work on this once they returned home.

Now the drums that were playing within the procession had stopped suddenly. The unseen drums from within Stonehenge began to slow and pound softly.

There were four very tall men. They were the ones carrying the deceased body and they continued walking until they entered the site through the wooden front entrance.

The remaining participants in the parade stopped. The outside crowd also stopped moving and remained standing. Some began to sit. Everyone was silent.

Ajax was fortunate enough to have been corralled by the crowd towards one of the spaces between two of the outer trilithons.

This opportunity allowed her a wonderful view to the inside of the monument, a view that most of those folks around her will not see; at least not tonight anyway. And it was not if she had a choice to move to either side either, because large people were directly on her right side and on her left side as well as those standing behind her.

Her view was astonishing though.

She was standing on one side opening that allowed her to see forward and directly to the center of the site as well as to her left and right a little. To her right she could see the large wooden front entrance.

Unable to move, Ajax just watched and took mental notes of what she was witnessing. She wanted to absorb and remember as much as she could.

She so wished that she had a camera or a notepad.

Suddenly, all drums had silenced from within Stonehenge.

She watched as the four tall men that carried the deceased body stopped short just before entering completely.

The Druid priest in charge slowly walked up to the four men.

"He must be the senior priest", she whispered out loud.

The priest raised up a short staff that he held in his left hand and then in his right hand held up something smoldering. "Maybe this was herbs and spices." Ajax thought.

The four men then lowered the body that was on the gurney, but stopped before the body touched the ground.

Ajax could hear the priest speak, but she could not make out the words being spoken.

The priest waved the short staff over the body followed with waving the incense. He then  lifted both of his arms straight up and then lowered his staff and the incense. With a nodding of his head, he slowly turned and walked toward the center stone in the middle of Stonehenge.

Many of the people in the crowd tried shifting their heads in attempt to catch a glimpse of the ceremony being conducted inside.

The four men then lifted the gurney back to shoulder height and proceeded to take their positions inside the site. They were only allowed to place the gurney onto and across the flat alter stone in the center of Stonehenge.

Ajax watch as events continued. Alexander remained quiet. He saw no need to interrupt Ajax as she witnessed how Stonehenge was being used at this particular moment in history.

Ajax continued to watch the event unfold. As it did, she also thought about where this procession of people might have come from originally.

"Where did all of this start?" She questioned.

She had read and heard about another place called, Woodhenge. It was located just a couple of miles to the northeast of Stonehenge.

It is believed by some that the purpose of

Woodhenge was that it represented life. It was made from the logs from trees and consisted of six or more concentric circles with one hundred and sixty-eight posts as well as having two standing stones.

Woodhenge represented life or new. It also may have originally been covered with cloth tarps stitched together or even interwoven tree branches. No one really knows.

She thought more of tonight's ceremony and that the beginning of today's celebration must have started two miles away at Woodhenge. It was a celebration to a life as well.

The conclusion to the all-day event would finish here at the cold stones of Stonehenge, representing death and finality.

But this was also the celebration to the winter's solstice sun rise and that this celebration must represent a new beginning as well. Maybe it was a way to guide the deceased to the afterlife or something or somewhere else.

How marvelous it was she thought to be so fortunate as to observe these things in real time, well, in their real time and her real time, wait. What? Okay, now this was getting real confusing.

Ajax decided to let the thought of this time travel thing go once again. It was just too deep of a subject for her right now.

Ajax's mind began to wonder again. She wondered how this event originally started and she wished that she was there at the beginning too.

She thought of what may have occurred there at Woodhenge.

Probably at sunset the night before, they began their preparations for the following day. Everyone would be dressed in bright clothing and would be cheering and celebrating new life. There would be happy celebrations around the land.   They would also have prepared the deceased for the trip to Stonehenge this day, December twenty-first.

Though it would be a cold morning, the villagers probably set great fires outside to warm themselves and the area around Woodhenge.

Woodhenge itself would glow brightly on the outside reflecting the glow from all of the fires like a great beacon of hope and anew brightness radiating from the earth.

She also thought that even though the day would end solemnly at Stonehenge, the next morning with the early morning's sun would renew the old, the past, and then the sunrise would bring to them a new day and a successful year to follow.

Slowly Ajax's mind returned to the events happening in front of her right now at Stonehenge as she took another look inside.

The priest had both arms raised to shoulder height. From the torch lights around him, his face glowed from inside the shadowed hood that covered his head.

This reminded Ajax of when a person shines a flashlight up from under their chin at night. It was kind of creepy. His robe sparkled and glistened from torchlight reflecting bright shards of light from the ornaments woven within the garment.

The body was now lying across the center stone.

The priest seemed to be blessing the body and preparing it for the afterlife ritual.

The four men who originally delivered the deceased remained silent and were kneeling on the ground around the alter. They were spaced ninety degrees from one another. As if they were marking the north, south, east, and west.

They were looking outward from the center stone where the body lay.

Ajax tried to look into the hood of the one facing her, but his face was totally hidden deep inside the hood. She could not even see a nose peeking out and she never saw his breath stream out from his hood.

"Creepy," she thought.

She also watched two other younger men assisting the priest as he performed several movements while continuing to speak. They scuttled around him, fetching this or that from hidden sacks.

She could not make out the words he was speaking.

Ajax took a quick look behind her and saw many people kneeling and praying while others were seen standing with their arms stretched upward towards the sky.

Her mind wandered and she wondered what time it was.

And just as she thought this, suddenly the drums from within the sanctuary began to pound softly, slowly, deeply.

The sound of, "tom, tom, tom," broke the silence outside the sanctuary.

A chill shuddered up through her as she turned herself back around to face the inside again.

The priest had stopped his ritual and the four large men had the stretcher lifted up once again on their shoulders. The body was tightly wrapped in shrouding.

As the drums played a rhythmic slow marching beat, the four men slowly carried the body out through the rear of Stonehenge where a handful of people stood waiting. These must be actual family members of the deceased.

This small entourage followed the four men. No others from the crowd had joined them. Soon, the small group had slowly walked out from sight.

They were probably heading towards the deceased's prepared grave site.

Ajax thought there was no need for her to follow them and observe the burial. It really wouldn't be her business and because she had come here to visit Stonehenge.

Unexpectedly, she noticed the drums were playing loudly and fiercely.

The people that were on the ground were rising up on to their feet, some even leaping up.

Drums from within the site as well as from all around the outside of the monument thundered loudly now. The sounds of flutes and clapping echoed around where Ajax stood.

She whispered, "What?"

She was taken by surprise and wondered what was happening. She thought that this was a solemn event.

But, the noise, the cheering, the thundering poundings from the drums continued.

Suddenly, Ajax's eyes caught sight of the eastern sky. Above the horizon, the sky was bright orange and yellow and mixed within a light blue haze.

And then she saw it. It was the leading top of the sun as it slowly crept up over the shadowed horizon.

The people erupted in cheers and yells.

Beams of the early sunlight shot out from the brand new sun and into the sanctuary. The sunlight ignited brightness from the stones that radiated within Stonehenge.

Ajax looked around and saw that everyone was now happily dancing and clapping. They were in celebration of the new day that brought them hopes for a full new season for planting and harvesting.

She realized how great a moment this was to these people that lived their lives based upon the heavens, the sun, and the moon.

Ajax's emotions soon shifted from being somber into jubilance. She even found herself jumping and leaping and dancing with those around her. Smiling and laughing wildly and humming along with the crowd as she held Alexander tight.

Wow, she thought. How great is this?

The morning continued on for quite some time with all of the people in constant celebration. Children were running around carrying long colorful streamers. Adults were seen drinking and eating.

Finally, in time, some of the crowd had dispersed, but many still remained for the celebration.

"I could stay here longer; Alexander, but we should probably head back home." Ajax said.

Alexander replied, "When you are ready, we will leave."

The two of them slowly walked away from the site stopping just before they reached the outer henge. No one seemed to notice them. They were all too preoccupied in celebration.

Ajax paused and spent several more minutes just observing and watching all that was happening, the people, the party, and most of all, Stonehenge as it stood majestically in the distance.

With a sigh Ajax said, "Okay, I'm ready."

And before she had finished speaking the word ready, they were gone.

Ajax's room lit up brightly. Slivers and stars of multi colored lights twinkled and bounced all around.

There sat Ajax on her floor holding Alexander. Her back was resting against the side of the bed as if she had never moved.

She whispered to Alexander, "That was totally great!"

Alexander did not respond, but remained silent.

She asked him, "How come I am always sitting when we return and that I am not standing as when we leave these adventures?"

Alexander replied, "This is because when we left this time here, you were sitting. If we had left while you were standing, then that is how we would return."

Ajax thought about it a little and nodded.

Suddenly, Morpheus darted out from underneath her bed and he quickly leaped up onto Ajax's bed. His eyes were locked onto hers and staring deeply at her. He walked very slowly towards her face which was at the side of her bed. His stare never moved from her eyes.

Holding Alexander tightly and out of sight on her lap, Ajax softly chuckled and then thought, "Oh, oh." But then she quickly realized that Morpheus is just a cat.

He can't do anything or tell anyone....

...he's just a cat.